New Pen Pals

by Cameron Macintosh

illustrated by Cheryl Orsini

OXFORD
UNIVERSITY PRESS
AUSTRALIA & NEW ZEALAND

T0362632

"I have some exciting news," said Mrs Andrew to her class one morning. "You have all been matched with a pen pal in Japan."

"What's a pen pal?" asked Matthew.

"A pen pal is someone that you write to, in a faraway place," said Mrs Andrew. "You can tell them about where you live."

"That sounds like fun!" replied Matthew.

"When I was your age, pen pals posted letters to each other," said Mrs Andrew. "Now, most pen pals use email."

Then Mrs Andrew told Matthew that he would be writing to a boy called Koji.

Matthew wanted to write to Koji right away.

He thought for a while, then he started typing on his computer.

To: koji@mymail.jp

From: matthew@schoolmail.com

Subject: Hello

Hello Koji,

I'm Matthew, your new pen pal!
Here is a photo of me, so you
know what I look like.
I live with my dad and my
older brother, Pete, on the sixth
floor of an apartment block.
I love to draw and play computer
games.
What do you do for fun?
From Matthew

Send

Ping! Matthew's email popped up in Koji's inbox. Koji read it right away and began writing back.

New Message

To: matthew@schoolmail.com

From: koji@mymail.jp

Subject: Re: Hello

Hi Matthew,

It was wonderful to read all about you.

Here is a photo of me!

I live with my parents. We live by a lake near a very big mountain called Mount Fuji.

I'm glad that you like computer games, because I love them too!

What games do you like best?

I hope to hear from you again soon.

From Koji

Send

Matthew was very excited to hear back from Koji. That night at home, he wrote back to him.

To: koji@mymail.jp

From: matthew@schoolmail.com

Subject: Games

Hi Koji,

The computer games I like most are car racing games.

My brother Pete loves them too.

We race each other most nights.

Dad sometimes tells us to be quiet because we argue loudly while we race!

What kind of games do you like?

Your pal, Matthew

Send

The next day at school, Koji and his classmates checked their emails. "I've got another email from Matthew!" said Koji, excitedly.

New Message

To: matthew@schoolmail.com

From: koji@mymail.jp

Subject: School Play

Hi Matthew,

I like racing games too, but I like treasure hunt games the best.

I have not had much time to play lately though, because at school we are working on a play.

I have the main part, acting as a jellyfish! My costume is going to be so cool.

It's great fun, but we have rehearsals after school each day, so I have been very busy. Do you do plays at your school?

Koji

Send

11

To: koji@mymail.jp

From: matthew@schoolmail.com

Subject: My school

Hey Koji,

We perform plays too. This year, our class will do a play about a bird that flies to the moon.

I hope to play the bird! Here's a poster for the play.

What is your school like?

In our classroom, we sit around tables. We sometimes work in groups with other kids. Here is a photo of my classroom.

From Matthew

New Message

To:	matthew@schoolmail.com
From:	koji@mymail.jp
Subject:	Cooking class

Hi Matthew,

Your school looks quite like ours, but I sit at my own desk, and our desks are in rows.

We don't do much work in groups, but Miss Go makes school fun.

She shows us how to cook lots of healthy foods. We made sushi today. We got to eat it too!

Your pal, Koji

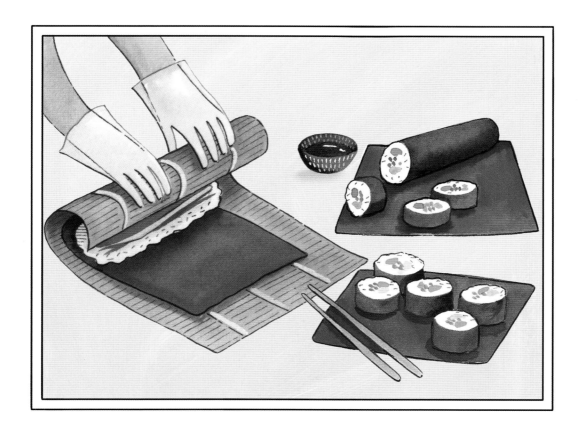

New Message — ✕

To:	koji@mymail.jp
From:	matthew@schoolmail.com
Subject:	My home

Hi Koji,

Your school looks great. I wish my teacher, Mrs Andrew, would show us how to cook!

What is your home like? Mine is not very big, but I like it anyway.

I share a bedroom with my brother Pete.

If we want to play outside, we go to the park.

Here is a photo.

Your pal, Matthew

New Message

To: matthew@schoolmail.com

From: koji@mymail.jp

Subject: Fish

Hi Matthew,

My home is small too, but I have my own room.

Here is a photo of my fish. They live in my room.

I have ten fish, in many different colours.

Do you have pets too?

From Koji

 Send

To: koji@mymail.jp

From: matthew@schoolmail.com

Subject: Honey

Hi Koji,

I like your fish! I have a cat who would like them, too!

Her name is Honey.

What is your town like? There are lots of apartment blocks where we live.

This is what I see when I look out my window.

From Matthew

To: matthew@schoolmail.com

From: koji@mymail.jp

Subject: Mount Fuji

Hi Matthew,

Your cat is very cute!

My town is small, but it's on the shore of a big, calm lake.

I have a beautiful view of the lake and I can see the mountain, too.

In winter it is usually covered in snow.

I hope you can visit one day! We can explore Mount Fuji.

From Koji

New Message

To: koji@mymail.jp

From: matthew@schoolmail.com

Subject: Visit

Hi Koji,

Wow, I love your lake and mountain. It's so different from my town.

I hope I can come and meet you there one day!

I want you to visit me, too.

From Matthew

Send